Happy Within
ありのままが幸せ

By Marisa J. Taylor
Illustrated by Vanessa Balleza

BILINGUAL
English - Japanese

I love the color of my skin. I am unique and beautiful within.

わたしはじぶんのはだの色がだいすき。たった一人のわたし、ありのままのわたしがすき。

I take pride in who I am and what I can do.

わたしでいること、わたしができることにじしんを持(も)っているの。

Being me makes me happy from within.
わたしでいられることに幸せ(しあわ)をかんじるの。

I love to sing, dance and play with my Friends, but that is just me. That makes me happy.

わたしは、うたったり、お友だちとあそんだりしてる時が幸せ。

What about you? What makes you happy?

あなたはどう？何(なに)をしているときが幸(しあわ)せ？

Some of my friends love to play with toys and make a lot of noise. That is okay too, because to them it brings joy.

あるお友(とも)だちは、おもちゃであそんだり、さわいだりするのがすきなんだって。それもいいね。

Some of my friends love to sing, dance and chat away. That's okay, because everyone is different and special in their own way.

ほかのお友だちは、うたったり、おどったり、おしゃべりするのがすきなんだって。それもいいよね、だってすきなことって、みんなそれぞれちがうでしょ!?

I do my best to be the best version of me.

だからわたしはじぶんらしく、そしてさいこうのじぶんでいられるようにがんばる。

I do not compare myself to the other children I see. I am proud of who I am and free to be me.

ほかの子(こ)とくらべたってしょうがないでしょ!?大切(たいせつ)なのは、ありのままのじぶん。

Some children will say things and make you feel sad.

だれかがあなたをかなしませるようなことを言(い)うかもしれない。

Don't pay attention to their words and continue to be glad.
でも気(き)にすることなんてないよ、笑(わら)っていて。

Let's support one another to be the best we can be.

みんながじぶんらしくいられるように助(たす)け合(あ)おう。

Everyone is unique in their own special way.

あなたってそんざいは一人(ひとり)だけ。それだけでとくべつなことなんだよ。

Be happy with who you are and what you see.

じぶんでいられること、じぶんだから感じられることを、
大切にしよう。

It doesnt matter where in the world you are from, nor the color of your skin. BE YOU and do what makes you happy from within.

どこから来(き)たか、はだの色(いろ)なんてかんけいない。あなたらしく、あなたが楽(たの)しいと思(おも)うことをしよう。

The moment you feel the butterfiles insdie and have a smile on your face, do more of that to make you grin.

心がおどるようなこと、えがおになれることをもっとやろう。

One thing to remember in order to be happy from within...

もっとじぶんをすきになれるよう、これだけはおぼえておいて。

Look at yourself in the mirror and say out loud 'I am the best version of me and happy within my skin'

かがみの中のじぶんを見て、大きな声で言ってごらん。「わたしはさいこうよ!」って。

If you believe in and love yourself, you can achieve anything and win.

じぶんをしんじて、そしてすきでいて！あなたにできないことなんて、なにもないから！

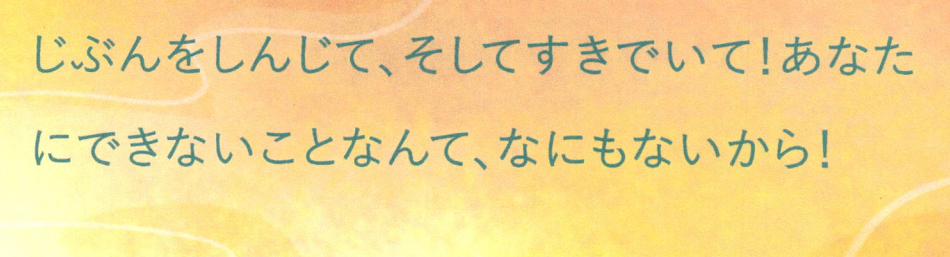

DEDICATION

This book is dedicated to all the children of the world. I made this especially for you so that you are reminded of how amazing you are. Never stop loving yourself, because self-love is the key to happiness.

Special thank you to my daughter Havana and husband Andre for inspiring me to write this. Thank you Naliya for giving me all the happy vibes allowing me to finish writing this book while you were in my belly. Extra special thanks to the most amazing and supportive husband, you are the best thing that happened to me. I love you more than words can describe.

Last but not least...Thank you very much Vanessa for understanding my vision and for bringing it to life through your beautiful images. ¡Muchísimas gracias!

This book is dedicated to Oreofe. Thank you for being part of Havana's life. The world needs more positive books representing amazing, loving and happy boys like you. We love you and your brother dearly.

Being me makes me....

....

What about you?
What makes you happy?

Happy Within
ありのままが幸せ
<small>しあわ</small>

Copyright © Lingo Babies, 2021

Written by Marisa J. Taylor
Illustrations: Vanessa Balleza

ISBN: 978-1-8382473-4-8 (paperback)
ISBN:978-1-914605-26-0 (hardcover)

Graphic Design: Clementina Cortés
Translation by Seiya Nobuta

All rights reserved. No part of this book may be reproduced or used in any matter without written permission of the copyright owner.

Marisa Taylor

Marisa lives in London UK with her husband and two daughters. They are a mixed Jamaican, Canadian & German family. London has a diverse range of people, cultures & ethnic backgrounds. However, she still found it difficult to find books that represent kids from all over. She is passionate about learning & teaching languages as it is a key element to connecting with people from other cultures. Her desire is to inspire and motivate children from all nationalities & backgrounds to love who they are and help provide resources to be happy within.

To learn more follow her on Instagram @lingobabies

Vanessa Balleza

Illustrator of children´s books based in Florida, Vanessa is passionate about story telling and teaching using her talents to help instil positivity. She has a beautiful and incredible ability to capture anyone´s vision and bring it to life with art, by adding her unique touch of imagination.

To learn more follow her on Instagram @vanessaballezaa

Ingram Content Group UK Ltd.
Milton Keynes UK
UKHW052237190623
423719UK00002B/12